THE ROUTE TO FINANCIAL SUCCESS

Unlock The Secrets to Financial Success and Achieve Your Millionaire Dream

BY

Danny M. Bryant

The information provided in this document is intendant to serve as general guide on the topic of success. While every effort has been made to ensure the accuracy and reliability of the content, the author and publisher make no representations or suitability of the information provided.

Table of content

CHAPTER 1

Introduction

We've all wanted to take a lot of vacations to far-flung places and spend a lot of money on the luxuries we've always wanted. In any case, the odds are good that you're surrendered to this never turning out to be in excess of a fantasy.

Notwithstanding, turning into a tycoon isn't as troublesome as you would suspect. Every year, a lot of people show that you don't have to be a banker or have a lot of money to make it to the seven figures.

Along these lines, here's our definitive manual for getting your hands on that million by 30. How about we get rich?

What makes a millionaire?

We should begin with somewhat of a disclaimer: 1,000,000 pounds simply isn't what it used to be.

It's getting more straightforward to turn into a mogul with each day that passes, because of things like expansion. Furthermore, for the overwhelming majority of maturing rich-listers, being well off is more an issue of way of life and not stressing over your funds, than the number in your financial balance.

You don't actually need a million pounds in your bank account to live like a millionaire. the vast majority of 'tycoons' don't. In any case, to really be a tycoon, you must be on top of your funds and ventures!

Being a tycoon can mean a wide range of things. In this aide, we're basically going to outline a sensible way to create your financial stability past £1,000,000.

The most effective method to turn into a millionaire

Here are our top ways to turn into a millionaire:

1. Set goals:

The cash game is a long trudge - cash doesn't develop on trees. Before you set out on your mogul challenge, you should have an unmistakable life plan. On the off chance that you're significant about this, you really want to know how to accomplish it, not simply dream it!

You must devise a viable and attainable strategy for making millions. While doing so, draw on your abilities, experience and desires.

With regards to laying out pay objectives, contemplate when you might want to resign. Most retired people are 'beneficiaries' since they're living off of their annuity which basically takes care of living expenses. However, you need to live like a tycoon, correct?

To get to this degree of pay without working requires genuinely sizeable benefits, in addition to a lot of different floods of automated revenue being procured consistently on your capital resources.

If you have any desire to truly party hard post-work, put forth a pay objective before you resign that doesn't expect you to work any longer.

This number will fluctuate for everybody, except anything it is, pick one and work to it. Rather than resigning at 70, you could find you're ready to resign at 58 in light of the fact that you've arrived at your objective.

When you surrender work, your venture portfolio turns into your pay portfolio. We carefully describe how contributing will assist you with turning into a tycoon beneath.

2. Financial plan consistently

Rehearsing some fundamental planning and cash-saving abilities at the earliest opportunity will place you in an advantageous position until the end of your life.

THE ROUTE TO FINANCIAL SUCCESS

Try not to simply discount it as 'something you'll do one more day'!

In the event that you haven't previously got it, download our free Understudy Cash Cheat Sheet. There are a lot of useful pointers there to help you get started.

Adhering to your spending plan takes discipline, however, the sooner you get into the tycoon attitude of purchasing resources rather than liabilities, the better. Most tycoons don't go around purchasing Lamborghini all the time while airing out the champagne at breakfast.

Truth be told, that is essential for the justification for what reason they're moguls in any case. Rather than sprinkling the money at each given an open door, they've permitted their means to develop.

That's what they say "A nitwit and his money are before long separated", and that is a genuinely fair maxim to live by to join the super-rich.

3. Begin straightaway

Time is a significant resource, particularly with regard to setting aside and putting away cash. So the sooner you start, the better possibilities you have of turning into a tycoon.

Utilize any extra time you have to make some money. Finding a part-time job is a good idea, but being more creative can also pay off.

Look at our fast methods for bringing in cash guide.

Or, if you have something to offer, why not start your own independent small business? Not only will this draw in some extra money, but, you'll try out your enterprising abilities before you've even graduated.

There's no keeping away from the reality you'll need to reimburse your Understudy Loan, yet not straight away. Dislike other obligations and won't influence your future objectives of rounding up truckloads of money.

What's more, you could find that occasionally you truly do have a couple extra quid, particularly when the credits come in. Start placing this into the investment account that sounds good to you. You'll be amazed how much premium you can acquire on it during your time at university.

Simultaneously, make sure to eliminate spending. Try not to have a vehicle and consider cautiously prior to sprinkling out on expensive things in the event that you don't actually require them.

4. Put cash in a tax-exempt ISA

One reason why individuals won't ever become tycoons is essentially in light of the fact that they don't have the foggiest idea how to.

There are bunches of contending choices out there battling for you to put resources into. You really want to think brilliantly and get your work done on what's accessible to you and what will give you the best return.

In the UK, tax-exempt money ISAs are one of the most mind-blowing approaches to developing your reserve funds reliably.

Why get a tax-exempt money ISA?

Consistently, every individual in the UK beyond 16 years old a recompense of cash they can place in a tax-exempt investment account, called an ISA. When your cash is in the record, it stays tax-exempt, Until the end of time. On the off chance that you don't go through your ISA stipend in a specific year, you lose that open door.

So if you have a touch of extra cash lying around, it merits contemplating placing it in an ISA. You can move to an alternate ISA supplier consistently if you need to, so search for the best rate. Typically, the highest interest rates are a few percentage points. So, if you put £20,000 into one of the best ISAs, you'll get tax-free interest for a few hundred pounds each year. You might contend that fundamental rate citizens get £1,000 of premium tax-exempt every year, so it's useless to open an ISA at this moment. A basic-rate taxpayer would still receive £400 if they invested £20,000 in a 2% savings account rather than an ISA with the same interest rate.

However, the future is the focus of this advice, not the present. Let's assume you sell your business, or get a critical compensation rise. Out of nowhere, you're not an essential rate citizen, and your tax-exempt revenue remittance drops to £500 or conceivably nothing, contingent upon your income. All that premium you're procuring will be burdened incredibly.

Thus, considering that there are no genuine disservices to keeping your cash in an ISA rather than a customary investment account and a few genuinely huge benefits, we'd say it's an easy decision.

For more on ISAs, read our aide on the best ISA accounts.

1. Always make an investment in yourself:

Quite possibly the most productive speculation you'll at any point make is putting resources into yourself. Also, we don't mean getting the costliest hairstyles and planner outfits. We mean putting resources into your abilities, outlook and information. Fostering your abilities can assist you with ascending the company pecking order and making automated sources of income beyond your work. Furthermore, dealing with your mentality and information around cash allows you to pursue better monetary choices that will set you up for a superior future. We have a rundown of books about cash to kick you off.

What's more, remember to take care of your body and brain. Making independence from the rat race is awesome, yet if your physical and emotional well-being is enduring, partaking in the mogul lifestyle is hard.

2. Find a job in an industry that you love and is lucrative:

you ought to attempt to get generously compensated graduate work. Having said that, give careful consideration to the career that you want to pursue: one that you will enjoy and be able to advance quickly in. Graduate schemes are frequently the best way to begin your career early with a high-paying position. Many organizations offer alumni compensations of £40,000 every year! On the off chance that you're finding it hard to get on the profession stepping stool, get a part-time job for now while you quest for new employment. Furthermore, on the off chance that you're truly battling to track down any paid work, don't hesitate for even a moment to sign on at the Particular Employment Place for a brief period.

3. Go into business:

The most optimized plan of attack technique for becoming wealthy in your twenties is to begin a high-development, exceptional-yield business with an arrangement to exit in no less than five years or something like that.

Yet there's positively no assurance you'll try and earn a cent, and the gamble can frequently offset your different choices for building a drawn-out pay. It's essential to have a well-informed thought and a strong field-tested strategy before you start, as well as a reasonable image of how you'll uphold yourself when there's no cash coming in. Having said all of this, starting your business career as a graduate is probably the best time ever. Your obligations are insignificant and regardless of whether everything turns out badly, you have an abundance of involvement to expand on and take forward. Ben Lebus began Horde Kitchen straight out of university and is a success among understudies, flaunting around 1,000,000 Instagram supporters!

Start with our list of business ideas if you're looking for ideas.

4. Utilize index-trackers to invest in the stock market.

On the off chance that you're curious about the financial exchange, it can generally appear to be a piece overwhelming. Over the long term, index-tracker funds consistently outperform the majority of actively managed hedge funds due to their simplicity. In basic terms, these assets are an aggregate venture that follows the developments of an entire monetary market.

Advantages of investing using index-trackers;

- Very inexpensive (automated trading eliminates costly traders)
- Requiring little knowledge of the market
- eliminates the need to choose the right stocks and emotions
- Simple to oversee on the web
- Can be held in a Stocks and Offers ISA for tax-exempt returns
- Expands the wizardry of progressive accrual (where the premium is made on revenue).

This kind of speculation works best when it's given quite a long while to appreciate and develop. Think of it as a long-term endeavour rather than a scheme to make money quickly.

Begin by perusing our aide on putting away cash.

Furthermore, to figure out how to make your millions utilizing this procedure, read Andrew Hallam's Tycoon Instructor (energetically suggested). If you're a finished beginner, you'll need to peruse our aide to make sense of how the financial exchange functions. Yet, recall that there is dependably a gamble while putting away your cash.

5. Divide out your earnings and capital.

Never keep all your investments tied up in one place. Throughout the long term, you ought to develop an arrangement of shrewd speculations that will get you set for when you resign.

A decent pay portfolio would preferably incorporate a blend of:

- Money and stock ISAs
- Government securities
- A benefits (private or state)
- Record tracker reserves
- Purchase to-let property (UK or abroad)
- Cash.

All of these are ways to keep making money. This sort of adjusted portfolio will pass on to you in a situation to partake in your retirement, as opposed to considering how you'll manage the cost of it. Furthermore, with the UK's state benefits deteriorating every year, that is an excellent situation to be in!

1. Get on the property ladder When renting a home, it's easy to think that every month you're wasting money. There are bunches of advantages to leasing. Yet, when you're somewhat more settled monetarily and you know where you need to reside long haul, it's really smart to begin contemplating getting on the property stepping stool. When you could be making monthly payments toward your own home, why continue putting your hard-earned money into the pockets of a landlord? You might be very cheerful living with your folks for a couple of years after you graduate and developing your money holds. In any case, whenever you've assembled enough for a store, now is the right time to begin house hunting!

Advantage of buying a property;

Whenever you've purchased your most memorable house or flat, you'll presumably be paying substantially less consistently in contract reimbursements than you had been working out on lease. What's more, you have a position of your special toward its finish.

By and large, property costs pursue serious areas of strength for a direction so you truly are putting resources into your future.

On the off chance that you're in a decent monetary position, taking into account purchase-to-let speculation is a subsequent stage to independence from the rat race.

Since you can get the underlying store down and get a decent home loan bargain that is not exactly the rental pay, you're on the road to success to being fairly rich.

Once more, you're probably going to profit from an ascent in by and large property costs. This implies you can acquire tons of money by selling at the pinnacle of the market and purchasing at the base.

There is the entire issue of getting a store together, and that is not exactly simple or easy.

Yet, the planning abilities you sharpened as an understudy will assist you with setting up an arrangement to set aside the essential sum.

2. Acknowledge your pension; **Retirement could appear like quite far off yet. However, it is very prudent to organize a pension fund before the age of 30. The advantages and of benefits developing your abundance are on a standard with file tracker speculations. Contributing even a small sum to a pension fund now can have a significant impact in the future. Keep in mind, that time is pivotal to receiving the rewards of self-multiplying dividends. Similarly, as with a significant number of different tips on this page, the key thing is to develop your insight into these significant kinds of speculation items accessible to you. On the off chance that you're utilized, you might get work environment benefits.**

3. Provided that this is true, look for insights concerning the supplier, as you're allowed to pick a superior or less expensive arrangement somewhere else.
4. Create a will; Keep in mind, whatever occurs, you can't take everything with you after you're gone. After a long period of saving and creating your financial stability, you believe that it should fall into the right hands when you're no more.

It very well may merit looking for proficient legitimate and burden guidance to ensure you have a methodology that boosts the recipients of your will. Also, don't wait until your grey; the earlier you start, the better!

How to legally become a millionaire in a short amount of time Above

we went through the lengthy but successful path to becoming a millionaire. That is, getting by on a very tight budget as an alumni and building an even and supported venture portfolio in your 30s onwards.

If that doesn't engage you, there are other more imaginative ways of turning out to be exceptionally wealthy in a more limited time span:

•   Move to another country - With a solid bank balance, you can live like an eminence in certain nations like India, Mexico and Thailand.

•   Lotteries, premium bonds, game shows and contests - This technique all comes down to karma. A punt, on the other hand, has paid off big time for a small group of people.

•   Profession decision - This guide has generally centred around effective financial planning. In any case, get into a lucrative industry or work and you may be driving the blaze vehicle speedier than you suspect.

•   Sell a business - We addressed this, however, there's something else to be said for firing up an organization, adding esteem, producing deals and flagellating it on.

• Matched betting: We don't recommend gambling because most people end up in debt, but for some, matched betting can be a quick way to big money. Look at our manual for matched wagering to benefit without risk.

• Property improvement - Increasing the value of houses is, unquestionably, an incredible method for creating financial stability moderately rapidly.

• Legacy - You likely haven't made a lot of decisions in this one. Be that as it may, you can continuously send a Christmas card to tragically missing well-off family members, for good measure.

1,000,000 isn't what it used to be, however giving you a truly agreeable lifestyle is even all that could be needed. Settling on astute speculation decisions will assist your money with going the distance. Whether you have two or three tanners spare, or maybe several thousand, give a serious idea of how you ought to manage it...

From zero to legend: 10 degrees that lead to millionaire achievement

you have obligations, your folks put their life reserve funds in you and you have dreams to accomplish. Whether you're at work or school, you're wondering, "How to get rich quickly?"

There is no one-size-fits-all quick fix for this, but there are some steps you can take to answer the question "How to get rich fast": I was rich quickly. On the whole, it's essential to comprehend the reason why you believe should do this — and whether you're doing it for the right reasons. Accelerating your path to wealth is a good reason to pay off debt. Numerous understudies and youthful specialists are much of the time in the red, and some of the time with unforgiving financing costs. You might be one of them. Regardless of whether you owe anything to a bank, you have a casual credit from your folks. An undergraduate degree can cost up to US$57,590, and it gets even more expensive if you want to study engineering, law, or medicine.

As an understudy living in the US, upgrade Abroad predicts you to spend up to US$28,000 every year on:

• convenience

- food

- transport

- service bills

- scholarly materials

That is on top of the country's expansion pace of around 3% for 2023. If you're overpowered by what you recently read, that is typical. You could try and be very much aware of this as somebody who wants to, as of now, or have concentrated on one of the most well-known concentrate on abroad objections.

Despite which point of your process you're in, knowing which degrees are better at addressing the inquiry *"how to get rich quick?"* is significant.

What's more, it's a lot more secure, legitimate and satisfying way to monetary freedom than questionable easy money scams, for example,

- Fraudulent business model: You will be approached by someone who wants to become an investor by promising you unrealistic returns from fictitious investments.

• Ponzi plan: By effective financial planning, you're guaranteed significant yields with next to zero gambles. Your cash is then used to take care of old financial backers, so it appears as though the plan is working.

• Fake opportunities for investing: Normally forcefully offered to you with apparently authentic records, you're approached to put resources into unfamiliar money, products, or even phoney organizations.

• Plans for multi-level marketing (MLM)

Since it is now so obvious what to stay away from, you can zero in on what works in the excursion of how to get rich quickly: trying sincerely and working savvy. Whether you want to, as of now, or have graduated, it's critical to realize what are the best degrees to assist you with addressing the inquiry "how to get rich quick?" so you can make good choices.

Before we continue toward the best degrees for you to succeed rapidly, how about we expose the glaring issue at hand?

CHAPTER 2

Step-by-step instructions on how to get rich as an international student?

Getting rich as a full-time undergrad would seem like a peculiarity, however, it's not generally as outlandish as it sounds. By and large, full-time understudies assume something like 12 acknowledgement hours for each semester, which is equivalent to four classes. You may have a lot of free time to work toward making money, but that will depend on the classes you take and how your schedule is set up. Even though you might be able to get a job in a fast-food restaurant or a retail establishment quickly, those aren't the best options if you want to make as much money as possible.

All things considered, here are a few open doors that can assist you with boosting your pay and assist you with getting rich as a full-time understudy.

Work as a Server in a Luxury Restaurant;

 If you live in a city with a lot of luxury restaurants and have a lot of experience serving customers, you can make a lot of money. For sure, the normal base compensation for high-end food servers in the U.S. is $16 each hour and $300 each day in tips.

Start Freelancing;

Make use of your skills to freelance to make money. Assuming you know how to compose well, look under the "Positions" tab on Prolonger for accessible composing open doors. As per for sure, the normal compensation for an essayist in the U.S. is $22.52 each hour, yet you can unquestionably make more.

On the off chance that you have different abilities, such as planning sites, altering recordings or making designs, you can pursue a dealer's record with Fiverr or promote your administrations on internet-based commercial centres.

THE ROUTE TO FINANCIAL SUCCESS

"Video/sound altering is a mind-blowing, profoundly attractive expertise," said Kelly Mosser, a planner and mentor for business people. " Whether you get contracted to alter somebody's web recording or assist a brand with refreshing its preparation recordings to be more current and drawing in, this is a help virtually every business will contract eventually."

Turn into a Confidential Guide;

As indicated by Tutor.com, the typical cost charged for mentoring is $50 each hour. In any case, on the off chance that you have some expertise in a subject, for example, assisting secondary school understudies with planning for the SAT, you might procure more. To amplify your pay, you could set up your own Internet coaching business and meet with understudies for mentoring meetings using Zoom.

Then, at that point, you will not need to burn through cash on fuel — and the time you save money on movement could be put toward more web based coaching meetings.

Register as a Virtual Assistant;

"Remote helpers bring in great cash supporting laid out web-based organizations, in addition to it's a mind-boggling brief training in maintaining a business," said Mosser. " You could advance more from its chiefs than you would in business college!"

The average hourly wage for a virtual assistant is $22, according to Indeed. Menial helpers offer far-off managerial or specialized administrations to entrepreneurs or different businesses. Managerial abilities could incorporate planning arrangements, composing and noting messages, accounting, overseeing online entertainment records or client assistance. Gaining practical experience in a speciality market can assist you with procuring more, as per for sure.

Serve as a Nanny;

If you go to a school in a huge city and have no less than one to two years of involvement working with kids, you could get a seasonal occupation as a babysitter. As per to be sure, the normal base compensation for a caretaker in the U.S. is $21.23 each hour. Notwithstanding, you could acquire more on the off chance that you offer extra administrations, for example, coaching, feast readiness or all-around arranged expressions and-artworks meetings.

Attend to Concerns for Other Students;

Assuming you have a specific range of abilities that most understudies don't have, you ought to use it to bring in cash. For instance, if you're splendid at settling PC issues, spread the word about it around the grounds, and individuals will reach you to help them. You can charge a demonstrative expense in addition to an hourly rate to chip away at tech issues. Indeed, reports that computer technicians in the United States earn $18.90 per hour. Regardless of whether you're not a tech marvel, there are different issues you could probably help settle for understudies and get compensated. Set aside some margin to conceptualize issues on paper that understudies have. Then, check whether any of those issues would be a way for you to offer your administrations and bring in cash.

What is the quickest method for getting rich as an international student?

Accomplishing your initial million a couple of years after graduating is conceivable. The initial step to figuring out how to get rich quickly, notwithstanding, is understanding that it requires a great deal of effort.

Numerous successful millionaires happened to be in the right place at the right time. It included:

- learning the scale on which tycoons work

- having the persistence to beat numerous disappointments

- pursuing great monetary routines

- being energetic about testing out ground-breaking thoughts

Figuring out how to take a gander at the excursions of fruitful individuals can be a critical consideration dominating how to get rich quickly.

Going to a similar college and picking a similar degree they canned put you at the perfect locations and ideal opportunity as well. All things considered, seeking a degree exclusively to get rich quickly may not be the best methodology, as monetary achievement is impacted by many elements past one's certification. Life's obstacles—love, family, and personal setbacks—can impede progress and are difficult to avoid. However, some degree's increase earning potential, and despite the usual obstacles, you can accelerate your journey on how to get rich fast. For this article, we'll utilize information from the US Agency of Work Measurements and decide the best degrees you ought to seek for speedy monetary achievement.

10 top degrees for rapid achievement in order to become wealthy quickly

1. Business Organization and The executives

This is one of the most adaptable and adaptable fields to study, giving you admittance to numerous jobs in numerous enterprises.

On the off chance that one job isn't working, you can move to another — and this is potential on account of 715,100 new positions that are to be made from 2021 to 2031. Having the option to move to start with one lucrative work and then onto the next expands your possibilities of getting more significant compensation. The middle yearly pay was US$76,570 in May 2021 — higher than the middle yearly compensation for all occupations of US$45,760.

2. Regulation

Legal advisors, particularly those who represent considerable authority in corporate regulation, licensed innovation, or case, charge continuously — and that implies the sky's the breaking point for those able to invest the hard effort to charge more. In the US, generally speaking work in regulation is supposed to become 10% from 2021 to 2031, which will make 833,100 new positions throughout the 10 years. The middle yearly pay was US$127,990 in May 2021. With each calling, you stand to acquire higher the more gifted and popular you are. "There are a lot of very wealthy legal counsellors, however, that is simply the top layer of the calling. According to Amanda Devereux, a partner at Cadwalader, Wickersham & Taft LLP, "most lawyers earn more of a solid middle-class income."

3. The Aviation Authority

To turn into an air traffic regulator, you want a partner or four-year certification from an Air Traffic University Preparing Drive (AT-CTI) program in the US, or a comparable expert in your nation of origin.

This will set you up to become answerable for the protected and effective development of airplanes in the air.

It's a task that is more enthusiastically than it looks as you want superb decisive reasoning and critical thinking abilities, as well as the capacity to remain mentally collected under tension.

In 2021, an air traffic regulator makes a yearly middle compensation of US$129,750. There are around 2,400 openings for air traffic regulators extended every year from 2021 to 2031.

4. Engineering

The interest for talented PC researchers is higher than at any other time — particularly during a time when tech organizations contend to send off the best web-based entertainment application. By and large work in software engineering is supposed to become 15% from 2021 to 2031. This increment ought to achieve 682,800 new positions throughout the ten years, a lot higher than different positions on our rundown.

5. Finance

For those of you who have a talent for adjusting financial plans and doing the math, a degree in finance holds a fair piece of commitment. As monetary investigators guide, you can direct organizations and people to pursue brilliant monetary choices.

The most outstanding aspect? In 2021, the BLS reported that the median salary for this position was US$95,570. By and large work in business and money is supposed to become 7% from 2021 to 2031.

Over the next decade, this increase should result in approximately 715,100 new jobs, significantly more than other jobs on our list.

6. Dentistry

Chasing after a particular clinical profession can be extreme, however, the prize merits the work. To turn into a dental specialist, for instance, you'll have to finish a five-year degree in dentistry supported by the Overall Dental Chamber, trailed by one to two years of postgraduate dental preparation.

At times, you are expected to finish a Dental Confirmation Test to be conceded into dental schools in the US and Canada.

That excludes the dental gear you'll deal with at university, the expense of clinical revolutions, or your cost for most everyday items as a worldwide understudy. The middle yearly compensation for this job, be that as it may, is US$163,220 in 2021. Generally speaking, work in medical care is supposed to develop by 13% from 2021 to 2031, which ought to achieve 2,000,000 new positions throughout the ten years.

7. Production network the board

A degree in in-store network the board is great for somebody who appreciates planning enormous-scope projects and figures out the requirement for thorough quality control boundaries. It's far superior on the off chance that you love the business in which these activities occur. You could likewise add to making supply chains more supportable and have your impact in battling environmental change. Generally, work in coordinated operations is supposed to develop by 28% from 2021 to 2021. The middle yearly pays for logisticians was US$77,030 in May 2021.

8. The board data frameworks

Huge information has been the greatest idea inside the tech space as of late. Taking on positions, for example, a data innovation project director, business frameworks expert, or even a specific programming designer are valuable open doors overflowing with potential. BLS predicts that work for PC and data framework supervisors will develop by 16% from 2021 to 2031.

9. Designing

A part of designing you can consider is polite designing. Engineers in this field are fundamental in planning and directing the development of foundation projects, like streets, extensions, and structures. This field extends to sufficient chances for lucrative positions— particularly in areas like development, transportation, and metropolitan preparation. From 2021 to 2031, employment of civil engineers is expected to rise by 7%.

Structural designers who succeed in their professions can progress to administrative positions, prompting expanded procuring potential. Some designing alumni wind up changing to different ventures, which is conceivable given the numerous adaptable abilities you gain. Because of this, the majority of engineering degrees will endure over time.

10. Online protection

As occupations in software engineering and the board data frameworks keep on thriving, areas of strength for seeing network safety professionals are to be expected. Accept filling in as a data security examiner, for instance. As a subject matter expert, you'll remain refreshed with the most recent security patterns, weaknesses, and countermeasures. You'll likewise perform risk evaluations and distinguish weaknesses inside an association's foundation, organizations, or applications. Information security analysts' employment is expected to rise by 35% between 2021 and 2031, much faster than the average for all BLS-listed jobs. The middle yearly compensation for data security experts was US$102,600 in May 2021.

10 cash decisions that assisted me with turning into a millionaire

There are generally 11.8 million Americans with total assets of something like $1 million, making up 3% of the U.S. populace, as indicated by Spectrum Gathering's 2019 Market Bits of Knowledge report. Even though it's no longer possible to be a millionaire, reaching that point is still a significant accomplishment. Before I turned into a millionaire at 28, I let myself know I was either going to make it or be an outright disappointment when I turned 30. The apprehension about having no work, no reserve funds, no speculations and no choice to resign early kept me roused. There is no "secret formula" for wealth accumulation.

Yet, I can let you know that street to turning into a mogul is a lot more straightforward when you're in your 20s: You have more energy, fewer wards and little to lose. I was able to reach a $1 million net worth at the age of 28 thanks to these ten money rules:

THE ROUTE TO FINANCIAL SUCCESS

1. Keep on track in school

Loosen in school will not go anywhere. Your marathon-watching propensities will just damage your GPA. There are lots of individuals who graduate in the top 1% of their group consistently. Be one of them. You're paying a large number of dollars for your schooling, so why not exploit it? You can continue to demand that grades don't make any difference, yet it won't change the work market rivalry. While a few esteemed organizations will let you know that "GPA isn't the entire story," it doesn't mean they will not request your record — because accept me, they will. Graduating with a 3.78 GPA assisted me with finding some work at Goldman Sachs. Yet, it was difficult. I aggressively applied for jobs for six months and attended 55 interviews before receiving an offer.

2. Save until it harms

I was once an unfortunate understudy, so finding some work with reliable compensation caused me to feel rich. Yet, I kept living like an understudy for quite a long time even after my most memorable everyday work. I was able to save as much as I did with a lot of willpower and discipline. I didn't rationalize concerning why I wanted decent garments or another vehicle. To keep my living expenses low, I lived with a friend for two years in a tiny studio. That allowed me to save another 20% of my 401(k) cash flow and max out my 401(k) on a low salary. Attempt to save no less than 20% of your after-charge pay consistently, come what may. Keep in mind, on the off chance that you're not in torment from how much cash you're saving every month, you're not adequately saving.

3. Work hard and know where you fit in.

Working hard requires no skill at all. That's what I guarantee assuming you're the main individual in the workplace and the last to leave, you'll excel. Put in your time early and you can unwind when you're more seasoned. Will your public activity endure? Yes, a little bit. However, you're youthful, recall? Your energy is boundless! Right off the bat in my vocation, I got to work at 5:30 a.m. What's more, left after 7:30 p.m. I gleaned some significant knowledge, accomplished more and acquired the admiration of my companions. What's more, because my supervisor perceived my persistent effort and morals, I had the option to save my occupation during the 2000 website bubble burst.

4. Think about both forceful and moderate techniques

Putting resources into an S&P 500 list reserve is fine, yet to get rich quickly, I suggest making all the more high-risk wagers. You can land greater success for a little piece of your portfolio. Try not to go off the deep end and blow all your cash away, yet explore different avenues regarding forceful speculation methodologies. Like I said, when you're youthful, you have very little to lose. At the point when I was 22, I just had about $4,000 to my name. In any case, I put 80% of my cash in one stock and got a 5,000% return. A piece of it was karma. Yet, I properly investigated things, faced a major challenge and it paid off.

5. Make property your closest companion

Expansion is a monster. Make it an objective to claim a main living place when you know where you need to reside for the following five to 10 years. Assuming you put a 20% initial instalment on a home and it goes 3% up each year, that is a 15% profit from your money. At the age of 26, I paid $580,500 for a condo in San Francisco with two bedrooms and two bathrooms using a lucky win from one stock investment. The home loan has since been paid off and the property currently produces a constant flow of pay.

6. Live like you're more unfortunate than you are

The more extravagant you become, the thriftier and serene you ought to be. Too many young people spend money on things they don't need just to look good in front of their friends and on social media. Being young and poor is nothing to be ashamed of. Drive a modest vehicle. Live in a humble home. Try not to eat out each day. Try not to purchase garments you needn't bother with (because of Imprint Zuckerberg and Steve Occupations, wearing the same thing consistently is cool). And afterwards, be the unpretentious tycoon nearby. When I turned into a tycoon, I bought a six-year-old vehicle and drove it for the following 10 years. From that point onward, I rented a Honda Fit and drove it for a considerable length of time. I wear a similar relaxed active garments I wore in my 20s.

7. Begin a part-time job

You can bring in cash by working a regular work or by beginning a business. Even better, you can do both. Over the long haul, your side gig could transform into a major business that will produce much more pay than your regular work. I started Financial Samurai in 2009 as a way to organize the financial chaos. I had no idea how rapidly the website would expand. It gave me the self-assurance I needed to negotiate a severance package in 2012 and quit my full-time job permanently.

8. Establish a robust support network

To advance, you must establish as many allies as possible. It isn't sufficient to Be a diligent employee. You must engage with people, demonstrate interest in them, and win their approval. Your entire career will advance significantly faster once you have someone with significant power on your side. I generally made it a highlight to take a partner out for espresso something like one time per week. I was able to advance to vice president at the age of 27 by cultivating strong relationships.

9. Put resources into your schooling

Your cerebrum is your most noteworthy resource. Solid training is the most important thing you have, so continue to extend your insight — even after school. You can now learn almost anything for free thanks to the Internet. In the wake of finishing my part-time MBA program, I kept taking courses to keep awake to date with everything finance-related. I continued to write on Financial Samurai as a result of that, and the more I did, the more money I earned.

10. Monitor your advancement

How much cash you save is a higher priority than the sum you procure. I know lots of individuals who made millions and afterwards wound up broke a couple of years after the fact since they had no clue about where their cash went. Exploit free monetary instruments on the web.

Track your income, dissect your venture portfolio, compute your monetary necessities in retirement — simply keep steady over your funds.

Since 2012, I've been using a free online tool for managing my wealth. By industriously following my total assets, I've had the option to streamline my abundance without limit.

CHAPTER 3

Money Mind-set: How to Think About Money?

To succeed financially, it is essential to adopt a positive financial mind-set. A cash outlook is your arrangement of convictions about cash, which impacts the monetary choices you make and influences your monetary life. Setting aside cash and burning through cash mirror your outlook. Based on your previous financial mistakes, it may change over time as you get older, wiser, and more knowledgeable.

We should plunge further into the cash attitude and see the reason why it is pivotal for monetary autonomy and opportunity.

How Did You Form Your Money Mind-set?

The statistics we presented in this article don't look good for a reason. Pessimistic cash propensities push individuals toward obligation, expanding their apprehension about losing cash and letting completely go in different parts of life as well. We must first comprehend how the money mind-set is formed before we can comprehend the numbers and how to alter our perspective. The brain science of cash is one of many variables that can influence your cash attitude. It shows in how you behave when you have money—how you spend it, what drives you, and, ultimately, how you feel about money. Does money inspire confidence, fear, gratitude, or another emotion?

Furthermore, your childhood and past encounters likewise assume a critical part.

How you grew up and watched your folks discuss cash quite early in life and act with a particular goal in mind will mirror your ongoing convictions about cash and your capacity to change your cash propensities and modify your cash mentality.

Require one moment to contemplate how your folks dealt with cash in your family and how they managed obligation, become obligation free, or take care of bills.

All of this will assist you with acquiring a superior viewpoint on cash, and you will have an extraordinary beginning stage for really impacting your mentality.

Why Is It Vital to Have a Different Money Mentality?

This statement alone is reason to the point of changing your cash convictions, eliminating the blocks, and further developing your monetary prosperity. Be that as it may, we haven't arrived to furnish you with persuasive statements yet to tell you the best way to practically adjust your outlook. In any case, before we give you a couple of tips.

Did you have any idea that out of 10,000 tycoons, 97% accepted they could become moguls and genuinely trusted their prosperity?

What you accept will drive your conduct in all parts of life, not simply finance. For instance, you will sit down and write if you are convinced that you must write in a journal every day for ten minutes because doing so is good for your mental health. Assuming you see the beneficial outcome, you will take on the propensity over the long run.

Do you think positively or negatively about money?

You can't determine whether you want to significantly impact your cash outlook until you understand what a decent one resembles and how it varies from a terrible one. We'll assist you in answering that inquiry for yourself for certain assertions and questions.

Negative Money Mind-set

•   You partner gloomy sentiments with cash. Do you feel regretful or embarrassed when you burn through cash on yourself? Do you get restless when you contemplate what is happening?

• You hold that being wealthy is bad in and of itself. Do you feel that well-off individuals are voracious or materialistic?

- You accept that having cash is outside the realm of possibilities for you. Do you imagine that you'll always be unable to set aside sufficient cash to purchase a house or resign?

- You consider cash a scant asset. Do you store your assets and never squander them since you're apprehensive about running out?

Certain attributes will generally remain inseparable from having negative and restricting convictions.

If you feel any of the accompanying routine, it very well might be an ideal opportunity to reconsider your relationship with cash and impact your money mind-set.

- You feel like you're constantly destitute, regardless of the amount of cash you possess in the bank.

- You accept that rich individuals are avaricious and narrow-minded. This perspective makes an inevitable outcome - you won't ever become rich yourself on the off chance that you accept that abundance is terrible.

- You feel that cash is the base of all shrewd. This perspective places you in a casualty outlook and will keep you from truly assuming responsibility for your funds. Rather than survey cash as malevolent, take a stab at reviewing it as a device that can be utilized forever.

- You feel regretful when you burn through cash on things for yourself. This is a typical side effect of what's known as the 'broke outlook.' It is described by the feeling that there will never be sufficient cash to go around and that spending any money on oneself is paltry and reckless. Truly, you have the right to every so often treat yourself! Simply ensure that your spending is by your fantasy future.

Positive money mind-set.

A positive cash outlook is perhaps one of the main things you can do to make monetary progress.

It makes a significant difference. The following are some important characteristics of a good mind-set:

- You accept that you should be rich (not qualified for it)

- You get a sense of ownership with your own monetary prosperity.

- You comprehend that cash is an incredible asset to be utilized forever and not something to be dreaded or venerated.

- You realize there is sufficient cash for everybody to prosperously live.

• You repeat positive money mantras like "I am a Money Magnet" or "I attract Wealth and Prosperity" every day. You will undoubtedly achieve your financial objectives if you adopt a money-focused mind-set and use positive affirmations.

8 Ways to Develop a Better Money Mind-set

The majority of us have a love-hate relationship with money. Here are eight ways to change your mind-set about money.

We need a greater amount of it, however, we likewise feel regretful and fretted over the cash we have. If this sounds recognizable, now is the right time to significantly impact your attitude and make a suitable conviction framework.

As talked about, the cash outlook shapes your way of behaving and is the most important phase in making riches.

1. Investigate Your Objectives and Return to Them Day to day

We discussed laying out objectives and how that changes your disposition toward cash and assists you with switching the adverse consequences of stress. Having objectives at the forefront of your thoughts will assist you with settling on better choices that will emphatically affect your spending plan and your life as well.

2. Connect with others who have similar financial goals

Having goals may not be enough to increase your wealth or alter your spending patterns because, over time, our motivation dwindles and we give up the good habits.

That is the reason it is crucial to encircle yourself with individuals who don't have restricting convictions and are on the excursion to bring in a sizable amount of cash to fund their ways of life. You can find such individuals in our Cash School people group.

3. Pursue Choices While Not Pushed

Since you have clear objectives and others to help you, you will feel in charge of your financial plan and life. No more trepidation or superfluous pressure.

This will permit you to pursue better choices that will reflect positively, and as soon as possible, you will see your cash developing.

4. Try not to Choose not to move on - Spotlight on Your Monetary Future

Previously, you committed a few errors. There's no way to change that, and you need to acknowledge it. Learning from our mistakes in life and taking immediate action to improve the future are crucial.

5. Quit Contrasting Yourself with Others

Since your companion has another vehicle or an extravagant planner purse doesn't mean you want to spend pointlessly to keep up. Set your principles and stick to them.

Embracing an "overflow mentality" can assist you with battling the inclination to be envious of others, which we as a whole do at times, in any event, when we don't intend to. Gone against to the world view limited by fear, the overflow attitude intends that there are an adequate number of assets — for this situation, cash — for everybody.

6. Centre around What You Have some control over

One of the greatest cash botches is that we frequently centre around what we have no control over. Our financial strategy should not be affected by the rises in the stock market, the housing market, or commodity prices. You want to pay for certain things, however, you can't impact the costs or all that is happening on the planet at present.

7. Prudent spending is easier said than done.

Notwithstanding, you can spend cash astutely, and the most effective way to do so is to begin living underneath your means.

Because you spend less than you earn, this is a good first step because it forces you to stay out of debt and save money.

8. Learn and Extend Your Viewpoints with Mentors and Courses

Assuming you observe that your accounting records are causing you stress or tension, it very well might be an ideal opportunity to look for proficient assistance. Acquiring information and studying a subject will assist you with conquering snags.

A specialist can help you comprehend and change the idea designs causing you trouble. Cash outlook training is another choice that can assist you with making monetary propensities and accomplishing your fantasy monetary life.

Around here at Abundance Country, we make courses and instructing projects to assist with people's finances and their ways of life.

With The Right mind-set, the time has come to Begin Funding Your Way of life

Now that you know the influence of taking on the right mentality toward cash, you can begin putting resources into yourself and your future. A portion of the things we notice here might appear to be senseless from the outset, yet having major areas of strength for a mentality is the first and most significant stage toward progress.

Financial Risk Management

Monetary Gamble The board is the method involved with distinguishing chances, breaking down them and pursuing speculation choices given either tolerating, or alleviating them. These can be quantitative or subjective dangers, and it is the occupation of a Money through to utilize the accessible Monetary instruments to support a business against them. In banking, for example, the Basel Accords are a bunch of guidelines embraced by worldwide banks that assist in tracking, reporting and uncovering credit, promoting and functional dangers. There are a few unique kinds of Dangers that finance troughs need to represent before proposing speculation procedures, and this article covers a couple of them exhaustively.

Operational Risk

Operational Risk - as characterized by the Basel II structure - is the gamble of circuitous or direct misfortune brought about by fizzled or insufficient inner individuals, frameworks, cycles or outside occasions. It incorporates other gamble types, for example, security chances, lawful dangers, misrepresentation, ecological dangers and actual dangers. Operational risks, in contrast to other types of risks, are not driven by revenue, do not occur knowingly, and cannot be eliminated. The danger persists as long as people, procedures, and systems remain ineffective and imperfect. However, operational risks can be managed by acceptable risk tolerance in terms of financial risk management.

This is finished by deciding the expenses of proposed enhancements against their advantages.

Foreign Exchange Risk

Foreign Exchange Risk is otherwise called money risk, FX chance or swapping scale risk. It is caused when a monetary exchange is made in money other than the working cash - which is many times the home-grown money - of a business. The gamble emerges because of troublesome changes in the conversion standard between conditional money and working cash. A part of Unfamiliar Trade Chance is Financial Gamble or Foreign Exchange; how much an association's item or market esteem is impacted by surprising swapping scale variances.

Organizations whose exchange vigorously depends on the import and product of merchandise, or who have broadened into unfamiliar business sectors are more helpless to Unfamiliar Trade Chances.

Credit risk

Credit risk is the gamble that a borrower or client defaults on their obligations or exceptional instalments.

With acquired cash, notwithstanding the deficiency of head, extra factors, for example, loss of premium, expanding assortment costs and so on., when determining the extent of the Credit Risk, must be taken into consideration. Monetary experts use Yield Spreads as a way to decide Credit Hazard levels in a market.

One of the easiest approaches to moderating Credit Hazard is to run a credit and keep an eye on an imminent client or borrower. Other options include purchasing insurance, using assets as collateral, or having a third party guarantee the debt.

 A few strategies companies use to relieve Credit Chance emerging from non-instalment of client duty, is to demand settlements ahead of time, instalment on conveyance before handover of merchandise or to not give any credit extensions until a relationship has been laid out.

Reputational Risk

reputation results in the loss of social capital, market share, or financial capital, which is known as reputational risk. This risk is also referred to as reputation risk.

Notoriety Hazard is extremely challenging to foresee or acknowledge monetarily, as Notoriety is an immaterial resource. It is naturally attached to Corporate Trust and is the justification for why Notoriety harm can hurt an association monetarily.

Criminal examinations concerning an organization or its high-positioning chiefs, morals infringement, absence of supportability strategies or issues connected with the well-being and security of one or the other item, client or faculty are instances of what can harm a substance's standing.

Minor issues can now become global issues thanks to the growth of technology and social media. This has prompted blacklists as a type of buyer fight.

In outrageous cases, Reputational Hazard might prompt corporate. Thus, more associations are devoting resources and assets to all the more likely deal with their standing.

CHAPTER 4

How Risk Management Works

Risk is indivisible from return. Each speculation implies some level of chance. In highly inflationary markets, it can be very high for emerging market stocks or real estate and very close to zero for U.S. Treasury bills. Risk is evaluated outright and in relative terms. A strong comprehension of hazards in its various structures can assist financial backers with bettering comprehension of the open doors, compromises, and expenses associated with various speculation draws near.

Risk the executives implies recognizing and dissecting where hazard exists, and settling on conclusions about how to manage it. It happens everywhere in the domain of money.

For example:

- A financial backer might pick U.S. Depository securities over corporate securities

- An asset chief might fence their cash openness with money subordinates

- A bank plays out a credit and keeps an eye on a person before giving an individual credit extension

- A stockbroker utilizes monetary instruments like choices and fates

- A cash supervisor utilizes methodologies like portfolio expansion, resource designation, and position estimating to relieve or successfully oversee risk

Constant gambling the executives can assist with diminishing the opportunity of misfortunes while guaranteeing that monetary objectives are met. However, poor risk management can have serious repercussions for businesses, individuals, and the economy. The subprime contract complete implosion that prompted the Incomparable Downturn originated from a terrible gamble on the board. Moneylenders gave home loans to individuals with awful credit and venture companies purchased, bundled, and exchanged these advances to financial backers as unsafe, contract-supported protections.

Risk Management Techniques

Coming up next is a rundown of probably the most well-known risk in the executive's methods.

• Evasion: The clearest method for dealing with your gamble is by keeping away from it. A few financial backers pursue their venture choices by removing instability and hazard. This implies picking the most secure resources with almost no dangers.

• Maintenance: This methodology implies tolerating any dangers that come in your direction and recognizing that they go with the job.

• Sharing: This strategy accompanies at least two gatherings taking on a settled-upon part of the gamble. For example, reinsurers cover gambles that insurance agencies can't deal with all alone.

• Moving: Dangers can be given starting with one party and then onto the next. For example, health care coverage implies passing on the gamble of inclusion from you to your backup plan as long as you stay aware of your expenses.

• Misfortune Avoidance and Decrease: This strategy means that you find ways to minimize your losses by preventing them from spreading to other areas, rather than eliminating the possibility of risk. Expansion might be a way for financial backers to diminish their misfortunes.

Risk The executives and Instability

Venture risk is the deviation from a normal result. This deviation is communicated in outright terms or comparative with something different like a market benchmark. Speculation experts by and large acknowledge the possibility that the deviation infers some level of the planned result for your ventures, whether positive or negative.

To accomplish better yields, one hopes to acknowledge the more serious gamble. Likewise, a by and large acknowledged thought expanded risk implies expanded instability. While speculation experts continually look for and sporadically track down ways of lessening unpredictability, there is no reasonable settlement on the most proficient method to make it happen.

An investor's risk tolerance determines the level of volatility they should tolerate. For speculation experts, it depends on the resilience of their venture targets. One of the most usually utilized outright gamble measurements is standard deviation, which is a factual proportion of scattering around a focal propensity.

The process is as follows: Find the investment's average standard deviation by taking its average return over the same period. Typical dispersions direct that the normal return of the venture might be one standard deviation from the normal 67% of the time and two standard deviations from the typical deviation 95% of the time. This provides a numerical assessment of the risk. Assuming the gamble is decent they can contribute.

Risk The executives and Brain science

Conduct finance features the lop-sidedness between individuals' perspectives on gains and misfortunes. In the prospect hypothesis, an area of social money presented by Amos Tversky and Daniel Kahneman in 1979, financial backers show the misfortune revolution. They observed that investors place roughly twice as much weight on the agony of a loss as they do on the satisfaction of a profit.

Financial backers frequently need to know the misfortunes that accompany a venture as well as how much a resource goes amiss from its normal result. Esteem in danger tries to measure the level of misfortune related to a speculation with a given degree of certainty over a characterized period. For instance, a financial backer might lose $200 on a $1,000 venture with a 95% degree of certainty north of a two-year time skyline. Remember that a VAR measure does not guarantee that 5 per cent of the time it will be significantly worse. It likewise represents no exception occasions, which hit mutual funds Long Haul Capital Administration in 1998. The Russian government's default on its exceptional sovereign obligation commitments took steps to bankrupt the mutual funds, which had profoundly utilized positions worth more than $1 trillion. Its disappointment might have caused the worldwide monetary framework.

Be that as it may, the U.S. government made a $3.65-billion credit asset to cover the misfortunes, which empowered LTCM to endure the unpredictability and sell in mid-2000.

Types of Risk Management

Beta and Latent

One gamble measure situated to conduct inclinations is a drawdown, which alludes to any period during which a resource's return is negative compared with a past excellent grade. In estimating drawdown, we endeavour to address three things:

- The size of each regrettable period (how awful)

- The length of every (how long)

- The recurrence (how frequently)

For instance, as well as yet curious as to whether a shared asset beat the S&P 500, we likewise need to know its similar gamble. One measure for this is beta. Beta, which is also known as market risk, is based on covariance, a statistical property. While a beta greater than or equal to 1 indicates lower volatility, a beta lower than or equal to 1 indicates greater risk than the market.

Beta assists us with grasping the ideas of latent and dynamic gambling. The diagram beneath shows a period series of profits for a specific portfolio versus the market return. The profits are cash-changed, so the place where the x and y-tomahawks converge is the money-identical return. Defining a boundary of best fit through the information focus permits us to measure the inactive gamble and the dynamic gamble. The angle of the line is its beta. Therefore, a gradient of one indicates that the portfolio return also increases by one unit for every unit of increase in market return. A cash chief utilizing a latent administration methodology can endeavour to expand the portfolio return by taking on more market risk or on the other hand decline portfolio hazard by lessening the portfolio beta under one.

Alpha and Dynamic

If market or deliberate gamble were the just impacting factor, a portfolio's return would continuously be equivalent to the beta-changed market return. Be that as it may, this isn't true. Unrelated to market risk, a variety of factors influence returns. Speculation chiefs who follow a functioning system face different dangers and challenges to accomplish abundance returns over the market's presentation, including:

• Stock-leveraging strategies

• Country or sector selection

• Fundamental analysis

• Position sizing

• Technical analysis Active managers look for an alpha, or excess return, measure.

Alpha is the portfolio return not explained by beta, which is shown as the distance between the y-axis intercept and the intersection of the x and y axes in our diagram above. This can be positive or negative. As they continued looking for overabundance returns, dynamic directors open financial backers to alpha gamble, the gamble that the consequence of their wagers will demonstrate negative as opposed to positive. For instance, an asset chief might imagine that the energy area will beat the S&P 500 and increment her portfolio's weighting in this area. Assuming that unforeseen financial advancements cause energy stocks to forcefully decline, the administrator will probably fail to meet the expectations of the benchmark.

The Expense of Chance

The more a functioning asset and its administrators can produce alpha, the higher the expenses they will generally charge. For aloof vehicles like record assets or trade exchanged reserves, you're probably going to pay one to 10 premise focuses in yearly administration expenses. Financial backers might pay 200 bps in yearly expenses for supercharged mutual funds with complex exchanging techniques, high capital responsibilities, and exchange costs.

They may likewise need to offer back 20% of the benefits to the administrator. The valuing contrast between inactive and dynamic systems urges numerous financial backers to attempt to isolate these dangers, for example, paying lower expenses for the beta gamble accepted and focusing on exorbitant openings to explicitly characterise alpha open doors. The notion that the alpha component of a total return is distinct from the beta component is commonly referred to as portable alpha.

For example, an asset director might profess to have a functioning area rotation strategy for beating the S&P 500 with a history of beating the list by 1.5% on a normal annualized premise. The investor is willing to pay higher fees to obtain the manager's value, also known as the alpha. The remainder of the absolute return (what the S&P 500 itself procured) doesn't have anything to do with the supervisor's exceptional capacity. Versatile alpha procedures use subordinates and different apparatuses to refine how they acquire and pay for the alpha and beta parts of their openness.

Why Is Risk Management Important?

Risk the board is a vital piece of the speculation and monetary world. It requires financial backers and asset supervisors to recognize, investigate, and settle on significant conclusions about the vulnerability that accompanies arriving at their objectives. Risk The board permits people to arrive at their objectives while relieving or managing any of the related misfortunes.

How Can I Practice Risk Management in Personal Finance?

Risk management in personal finances can be practised through several different methods. Begin by recognizing your objectives, and afterwards feature the dangers related to your goals. Assess the risks and investigate the most effective strategies for managing them once you have identified them. You will probably need to screen and make acclimations to guarantee you keep steady over your objectives.

How Do Companies Manage Their Operational Risk?

Functional gamble is any gamble related to the everyday tasks of a business. Organizations can oversee it by distinguishing and surveying expected chances, estimating them, and setting up controls to either alleviate or dispose of them by and large. Companies must also keep an eye on their operations and risk management strategies to see if they are effective and make any necessary adjustments.

The Consequences Risk plays a significant role in the financial sector. The word frequently raises sensations of antagonism since there is the potential for capital and speculation misfortune. Yet, the risk isn't generally terrible because ventures that have more gambling frequently accompany the greatest prizes. Understanding what the dangers are, how to distinguish them, and utilizing appropriate gamble the executive's strategies can assist with alleviating misfortunes while you receive the benefits.